HOMOL'OVI: A CULTURAL CROSSROADS

William H. Walker

Arizona Archaeological Society, Homolovi Chapter, Winslow

About the Author

WILLIAM H. WALKER is an Assistant Professor at New Mexico State University in Las Cruces, New Mexico. He earned his Doctorate in Anthropology from the University of Arizona in 1996. While a graduate student he participated in excavations in the Homolovi Ruins State Park between 1989 and 1995, directing excavations at Homol'ovi II between 1993 and 1995.

© Copyright 1996 by the Arizona Archaeological Society, Homolovi Chapter

ISBN 1-889415-01-4

Printed in the United States of America by
Arizona Lithographers
351 North Commerce Park Loop
Tucson, Arizona 85745

Printed on 60# Halopaque Text -- a recycled paper.

TABLE OF CONTENTS

FOREWORD

It is early summer and the year is 1914. From the highest point at Homol'ovi, young *Humequaptewa,* now in his early teens, gazes upon the sights of the railhead called Winslow, Arizona. After running sixty miles and fording no less than five washes, *Humequaptewa* finds himself in the second most favorite place in his world: a promontory from which he can watch the spectacle of bellowing, monstrous locomotives and their long tail of rail cars. After the last train has left the rail yard, *Humequaptewa* makes his way back to the village and relates to his family everything he experienced on this day. His siblings never tire of stories of the noise, the smoke, the steam, and the strangely costumed men who attend to the locomotive giants. When they are older and stronger, they will accompany *Humequaptewa* on the 120 mile roundtrip run to the place called Homol'ovi and have stories of their own to tell.

I have heard many of these stories from my grandfather *Humequaptewa* and my great aunts and great uncles. Homol'ovi, which in Hopi view includes Winslow, has a very special place in the history and hearts of Hopi people across many generations. In this resource book, Professor Walker presents a concise history of the region's earliest residents as evidenced through the science of archaeology and the ethnological record maintained by Hopis and Hopi clans. The ebb and flow of life in Homol'ovi is also chronicled. For some, the archaeological record points to abandonment as a human response to climatic and environmental change and stress. Hopis, however, would say Homol'ovi was neither completely abandoned nor forgotten. It continued to attract Hopis who wished to retrace pathways of their ancestors and honor the site and spirit of the Little Colorado River that supported life and continues to support life in "Homol'ovi V" -- Winslow, Arizona.

The Homol'ovi region has been and continues to be a cultural crossroads for the many who pass through and the many who have taken up residence there. For some, including Hopis, it is part of the spiritual center of their universe. To others, it has offered opportunities for making a living and raising families. The railroad provided the most recent attraction. The ethnic diversity of Winslow is a marvelous blend of indigenous and immigrant populations who came to work on the railroad and, at the same time, established binding relationships with one another. Changes in modes of transportation, industry, and economy impact the ebb and flow of life in the region as they did in the distant past.

Humequaptewa, like others of his time, was so attracted to trains that he made a conscious decision to pursue a career with the railroad. For employment purposes, he assumed a new name, Ben H. Setima, and took up residency in Winslow. He had a long and successful career with the Santa Fe Railroad, married, raised a family and spent much of his free time meeting with and offering hospitality to passersby and newcomers to the Homol'ovi region. He was a true participant in the cultural crossroads known as Homol'ovi.

Hartman H. Lomawaima
Associate Director
Arizona State Museum
The University of Arizona

PREFACE

I first heard about Homol'ovi in 1980. A small article in an Arizona paper told of an ancient pueblo ruin being destroyed by illegal collectors. I remember thinking how sad it was that a few people could damage such an important part of our cultural heritage. Little did I realize that although the damage to Homol'ovi revealed the extent of greed in some people, it would also show the good that can be done when people work together for a worthy purpose.

The damage to Homol'ovi created a groundswell of concern and led to the Hopi people joining the people of Winslow and other concerned individuals and organizations throughout Arizona to work toward the establishment of Homolovi Ruins State Park. Through the efforts of these people and Governor Bruce Babbitt, the legislation establishing the park was signed in 1986 and by 1987 staff was on site protecting the archaeological sites while work began on developing facilities for visitors to Homol'ovi.

The intense interest in the park has created a rather unique situation at Homol'ovi. Representatives of the Hopi people and of the people of Winslow have been involved in all stages of planning and development of the park. The Hopi review park research plans, development plans, and educational materials. Because the park encompasses sites sacred to the Hopi people, I feel fortunate that the Hopi have been willing to work with park staff to develop an accurate presentation of the Hopi culture and its links with Homol'ovi and to ensure the protection of sacred sites and shrines throughout the park. One interesting result of this cooperation has been the large percentage of Native Americans who visit the park and who participate in our workshops.

I am quite fascinated by the reactions of visitors to Homol'ovi. Accustomed to seeing the large standing walls often found in National Parks, a few visitors look at our collapsed ruins and see only rocks and weeds. Most visitors, however, become fascinated with the story of Homol'ovi and hints these ruins give us of the lives and culture of the people who lived here. Homol'ovi provides an important link between earlier residents of the area and the Hopi people of today. By studying the Homol'ovi sites using proper archaeological techniques we can better understand the interrelationships of people with the land and the enduring ties of the Hopi with their ancestral sites. The archaeological excavations at Homol'ovi have, to an amazing extent, supported the oral traditions of the Hopi concerning their migration routes and history. With a land so steeped in history, it is sometimes difficult to understand how some people can fail to appreciate the importance of protecting and preserving Homol'ovi as well as other prehistoric sites throughout America.

In historic times, Homol'ovi has experienced a wide range of interactions with people, from the religious visits of the Hopi people to the visits of non-Indians wanting to learn about the history of this land; from the depredations of illegal collectors interested only in a showy piece of pottery to the archaeologist excited over ancient grains of pollen which reveal information about the environment and crops of prehistoric people. When you visit Homol'ovi you too will have an interaction with this land. It may only be a quick surface relationship with a glance at a ruin before you head on down the road, or it may be a far deeper relationship leading to a respect and appreciation for a land and a people who have much to tell us about living in the proper way.

Karen Berggren
Park Manager
Homolovi Ruins State Park

ACKNOWLEDGMENTS

A number of individuals and groups contributed their ideas and labor in making this work possible. Charles Adams, Karen Berggren, Cathy Johnson, Richard Lange, Mike Schiffer, and several anonymous reviewers from Arizona State Parks and the Homolovi Chapter of the Arizona Archaeological Society read several drafts of this booklet. I thank you all. Richard Lange, Charles Adams, and Ann Schmidt energetically helped me track down information and illustrations. Richard Lord, as usual, provided his time, film, and talent as photographer. Ron Beckwith did his customary excellent job drafting the figures. Arizona State Museum personnel who provided assistance included Alan Ferg, who kindly supplied historic artifacts for the cover; Ken Matesich, who took and prepared many of the photos; and Mike Jacobs and Kathy Hubenschmidt who helped in finding and preparing materials for the figures. Thanks also to the Hopi Cultural Resources Advisory Task Team for their insights and comments.

A number of institutions also provided their direct and indirect support of this publication, including the Arizona State Museum, University of Arizona; Arizona State Parks; Earthwatch; The Hopi Tribe; and the Homolovi Chapter, Arizona Archaeological Society.

W.H.W.

About the Cover

The cover is a composite of artifacts from the Homol'ovi area representing the span of human occupation here. The projectile points (for darts or spears) are from the Middle and Late Archaic and pre-ceramic Basketmaker periods (ca. 3000 B.C. to A.D. 500-600) and are made of chert and petrified wood. If the cover is opened flat, the gray and white pottery at the top center is from the early ceramic period occupations (A.D. 600-800 and on into the mid-1100s). The plain brown/red pieces date to about this same time period. The corrugated pieces date from around A.D. 1050 into the 1200s and 1300s. The orange and red sherds date from the 1200s into the 1300s. The yellow pottery is Jeddito Yellow Ware, imported down from the Hopi Mesas and dating to the 1300s. In the bottom left corner is bottle glass, marbles, china, ceramics, tokens, and other materials dating to the Mormon and later occupations at the site of Brigham City (after 1880). The photograph of these artifacts was taken by Ken Matesich, Arizona State Museum.

INTRODUCTION

If you look north from U.S. Interstate 40, as you cross the Little Colorado River you can see the ruin of Homol'ovi I as it was seen by U.S. Military Officers surveying here in the 1850s. This stretch of the river, known as Sunset crossing, is an area of high bedrock in the bed of the Little Colorado River. Prehistoric trails, stagecoach routes, the railroad, historic Route 66 and U.S. Interstate 40 all have crossed here to avoid the muddy river's numerous quicksand deposits.

The middle Little Colorado River Valley has been a cultural crossroads for thousands of years. If you know what to look for, the Homolovi Ruins State Park holds a wealth of historical and archaeological information. Seven ancestral **Hopi pueblos**, occupied between A.D. 1260 and 1400, are the namesake of the Park. Only the four in which excavations have occurred to date will be considered in any detail in this booklet. *Homol'ovi* (pronounced hoe mol' oh vee) is a Hopi word meaning "place of the little hills." These ancestral Hopi villages form part of a long history of prehistoric peoples who lived in the Four Corners region of the American Southwest for more than 2000 years.

The Homol'ovi **sites** have been the focus of an archaeological research project by the Arizona State Museum, University of Arizona, since 1984. This project, in cooperation with Arizona State Parks, Earthwatch, and the Hopi Tribe, seeks to understand how these ruins came to be here and the part they played in the rich history of Arizona. Ultimately, knowing the struggles and accomplishments of the builders of the Homol'ovi pueblos enriches the history of people everywhere.

Archaeologists ask: What happened in this region of the Little Colorado River before these pueblos were settled? That information sets the stage for exploring what life was like when the pueblos were occupied and also why they were eventually abandoned. To begin understanding this long historical process, archaeologists have closely studied the relationship between the local environment and the prehistoric Homol'ovi peoples.

The Little Colorado River, a central feature of the Homolovi Ruins State Park, has its headwaters in the White Mountains 165 miles to the southeast. As it flows to the northwest, it drops approximately 6300 ft (1920m) in elevation from its headwaters to its confluence with the Colorado River at 2725 ft (831m) above sea level. The floodplain of the Little Colorado River reaches its widest expanse--2.5 miles (4 km)--in the vicinity of the Homol'ovi ruins. The sandy loam soils on this floodplain would have been relatively fertile for prehistoric farming, as would the sand dunes that form on the terraces overlooking the river.

As it flows through the Homol'ovi area, the river is joined by shallow side valleys defined by low sandstone buttes and mesas as well as cobble ridges and terraces. Active and stable sand dunes cap the terraces and ridges to the north and east of the river. Each of these landforms provided particular resources (plants, animals, farmable soils, and raw materials) for the prehistoric inhabitants of Homol'ovi.

The lowest layers in the exposed buttes and mesas are known as the Moenkopi formation. This rock has a deep red color and is composed of fine-grained sandstone interbedded with occasional layers of silts and clays of red, green and yellow. Its exposed sandstone surfaces were favored locations for prehistoric rock art. Moenkopi clays were also used for construction materials such as plaster and mortar for pueblo walls and for the manufacture of pottery vessels.

The upper layers of the buttes and mesas are capped by the Chinle Formation. This geologic formation has several distinctive layers including, from bottom to top, the Shinarump Conglomerate, the Petrified Forest member, and the Owl Rock member. The Shinarump Conglomerate is composed of coarse, often poorly-cemented sandstone, as well as quartzite and chert cobbles. Surfaces of the Shinarump were also used for rock art. Many of the terraces and ridges that occur in the side valleys of the park were formed over millions of years as the Shinarump eroded--depositing these cobbles on the landscape. These cobbles were an important source of raw material for many of the flaked stone tools found in the Park. The Shinarump and the Moenkopi sandstones were also quarried for building materials and groundstone tools, like the **manos** and **metates** used to grind corn, clay, and minerals.

The Petrified Forest member of the Chinle formation contains distinctive clay deposits of various colors. The Little Painted Desert, located off State Route 87 about thirteen miles north of the Park, is a large exposure of these clays, and is a spectacular place to see as you travel through this area. Potters tended to avoid these clays, but they were used as mortar, roofing mud, and plaster. This layer takes its name from the large quantities of fossilized or "petrified" wood found in it. Petrified wood occurs in several forms; some is glassy and useful for making flaked stone tools. In the Park, however, it is more common to find white grainy pieces that do not flake well and were used as wall stones, hoes, or other tools. The Homol'ovi peoples, like their Hopi descendants, recognized that fossil stones were once living objects and, therefore, incorporated pieces of petrified wood and other fossils into their rituals. The Owl Rock member is exposed in the east end of the Park and was a prehistoric source of gypsum and volcanic scoria, materials occasionally used for making artifacts.

Mean temperatures along the Little Colorado River are relatively mild, averaging 28° to 32° Fahrenheit (-2 to 0°C) in January and 62° to 80° Fahrenheit (18 to 28°C) in July. However, in the Homol'ovi area, summer highs in the upper 90s and low 100s (38 to 40°C) are not uncommon. There are approximately 180 frost-free days in the Homol'ovi area, well above the minimum of 120 days required for corn farming or 150 days for cotton. Winter storms between December and March and convection monsoon rains, largely from July to September, provide the majority of the precipitation along the Little Colorado River. This well-watered floodplain and the fertile upland soils along this stretch of the river played a critical role in the region's colonization by the ancestral Hopi as well as later American settlers.

Although the temperatures did not fluctuate drastically in the past, the amounts of rainfall and water running in the Little Colorado River have been variable over time. Reconstructions of the climate indicate that between A.D. 572 and 1545 the area experienced several droughts as well as episodes of sustained rainfall. Between these wet and dry periods were years of more moderate rainfall. During the period from A.D. 1275 to 1300, the Homol'ovi area and the rest of the Southwest experienced a sustained drought.

Even during this very dry period the Little Colorado River would have been a running stream. As such it would have attracted people seeking sources of permanent water. During times of drought the floodplain would have been dry and crops could have been planted close to the river without fear of destruction by flood. During the wetter periods, fields would have been placed farther from the river along the margins of the floodplain or even in the sand dunes to escape the more frequent and severe episodes of flooding. Periods of moderate rainfall would have been less predictable and fields probably would have been placed in both areas. This would allow the prehistoric farmers to preserve at least some of their harvest in the event of an unexpected flood.

From ancient times the Homol'ovi area has been a place of immigrant farmers. Some of the earliest farmers in northern Arizona, the Basketmaker peoples, settled here for parts of the year to raise corn, beans, and squash. Later the large Homol'ovi pueblos were founded by immigrants from the Hopi Mesas to the north and others from the upper Little Colorado River area to the southeast. People lived in these villages year round, growing staples, like corn, in the sandier parts of the floodplain or in the fertile sand dunes. On the moist floodplain they farmed the prehistoric Southwest's most precious commodity--cotton. In societies without rare metals, fibers woven into cloth are often extremely valuable. Among the ancient pueblos of the Southwest, cotton provided materials for basic clothing and more importantly the ceremonial kilts, sashes, burial shrouds, and symbolic string used in pueblo rituals.

The **katsina** religion of the modern Hopi and Zuni pueblo peoples has its origin in the ancient villages found along the upper Little Colorado River. Peoples from those villages brought this religion to the Homol'ovi area where it continued to develop, making possible the construction of some of the largest villages in the Southwest. For a time these Homol'ovi pueblos prospered by controlling the floodplain, probably through irrigation. The cotton they grew was woven in their ceremonial rooms, known as **kivas**, and was a critical component of their ritual practices. It was also traded to other pueblo groups for similar uses.

The Mormon settlers of the 1870s also found the floodplain appealing and dammed the Little Colorado for irrigation. Although floods destroyed their crops and dams every year as spring and summer rains rushed down the river, they held out for four years. Like the pueblo peoples before them, these immigrants were fortified by religious zeal and only abandoned their settlements when officially released from their spiritual mission by Mormon elders in Salt Lake City.

Even later immigrants, such as those who built the Atlantic and Pacific Railroad in 1881, realized a golden opportunity in the transport of people and goods to and through this landscape. From a railhead in Winslow they could bring people and products by the thousands to the West and ship raw materials to markets in Kansas City, Chicago and other points east. This commerce created a city along the middle Little Colorado River. Winslow was born on the frontier of turn-of-the-century, industrial America and was home to rich businessmen, cowboys, railroaders, Hopi, Navajo, Chinese, African Americans, and numerous others. It afforded all the excitement of an early modern city including electric lights, an icemaking factory, an opera house, brothels, and gambling hall saloons.

It is the mission of the Homolovi Ruins State Park to bring to light the unknown histories of all these peoples, ancient and modern, who at different times for different reasons crossed this stretch of the Little Colorado and made it their home. The vast majority of that task involves the study of peoples for which there are no written records. Their story must be reconstructed through archaeological studies of **artifacts**.

THE CULTURE HISTORY OF THE PARK

Combining **survey** and excavation data, archaeologists have reconstructed a history of the Park. The history will be updated and enriched as archaeological research continues at the Park. Although prehistoric peoples have lived in this part of North America for at least the last 11,000 years, the Homolovi Ruins State Park has very little evidence of these very early peoples. The principal occupations identified by the Homol'ovi Survey occurred between A.D. 620 and 1400. This span of time has been divided into early, middle, and late periods, as follows:

The Early Period   A.D. 620-890
The Middle Period   A.D. 1000-1225
The Late Period   A.D. 1260-1400

The earliest settlers lived in **pit houses** (see Figure 1). Generally **sites** consisted of small groups of two or three families with each one occupying a pit house. A site comprised of a small cluster of pit houses is called a hamlet to distinguish it from a village, which is composed of larger groups of people. In the Park, eight pit house hamlets located in the gravel terraces overlooking the river date to the early period. Analysis of prehistoric plant remains has determined that they were cultivating corn and beans. These people supported themselves by farming in the sand dunes and the margins of the floodplain, supplemented by hunting and gathering animals and wild plants. Rabbit bones as well as the few deer or mountain sheep found in excavations indicate the kinds of game hunted during this time.

The Early Period peoples probably wintered in the warm pit houses, and planted their corn in the spring. During the summer months, hunting groups and perhaps others involved in ceremonial activities would have left the hamlets. It is even possible that those settlements were vacated for parts of the year. Those who stayed behind would have tended to crops and watched over the community. All would come back to the hamlets in the fall for harvesting the corn.

Seven pit house hamlets were inhabited within the Park area during the Middle Period. Like the earlier hamlets, these were found along the gravel terraces on the east flank of the river. These people also relied on a combination of wild and cultivated resources. In other parts of the Colorado Plateau during this time, people shifted to living in above-ground masonry houses or pueblos. Such early pueblos, however, have not been found in the Park. Instead, pit houses remained the primary architectural form at Homol'ovi until the mid-A.D. 1200s.

The history of the area changed abruptly about A.D. 1260 with the founding of the 150-room pueblo of Homol'ovi IV by people determined by their pottery and architecture to have immigrated from the vicinity of the Hopi Mesas. Approximately 20 years later several

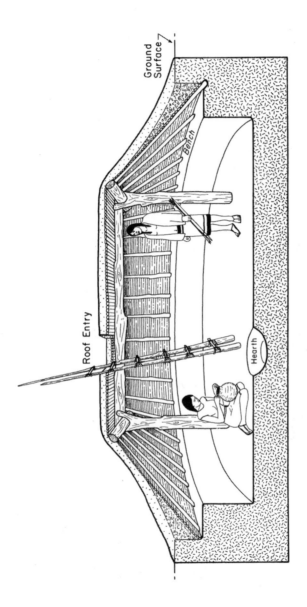

Figure 1. A Typical Pit House of the Early Period.

pueblos, including Homol'ovi III, Homol'ovi I, Cottonwood Creek, and Chevelon, were founded by immigrants from the upper Little Colorado region. Jackrabbit Pueblo, located 15 miles upstream and outside of the Park, is also associated with this immigration into the Homol'ovi area. The latest and largest pueblo in the Park, Homolovi II, was built in the A.D. 1330s by new immigrants from the Hopi Mesas. All of these pueblos were abandoned by A. D. 1400.

As a first step toward understanding the people who created this archaeological landscape over the past several thousand years, the Homol'ovi Research Program has concentrated on identifying the causes of the migration of large numbers of people into the area in the late 1200s and how the immigrants organized themselves in the large pueblos. Excavations have been carried out at the pueblos of Homol'ovi I, II, III, and IV.

LINKS WITH HOPI PUEBLOS

One of the most exciting aspects of this research program is exploring the similarities and differences between these large 14th century pueblos and the historically known Hopi pueblos. This comparative research allows archaeologists working in the Park to draw upon a great amount of information to enrich their interpretations of the Homol'ovi Ruins.

For example, the modern Hopi pueblo of Walpi resembles a stone-and-mud apartment complex arranged around several open spaces known as **plazas**. Pueblo rooms at Walpi are constructed in a terraced fashion, one on top of another, in some places reaching three stories high. There are also underground structures, usually in the plaza areas, called **kivas**. These kivas are used in religious ceremonies as well as for meeting places where men can gather in their free time to socialize.

At Walpi, households of related women, their husbands, and children live in a series of adjoining rooms on several floors of the pueblo. These households occupy several rooms, linked by open doorways, that are used for living quarters, different types of storage, the grinding of corn and sometimes ritual activities. Rooms facing the plazas are usually living spaces or habitation rooms. In the past such habitation rooms were entered through hatchways in their roofs, but today they usually have doors. Habitation rooms usually have sleeping quarters, a fireplace, and domestic tools, such as cooking pots, storage vessels for water and food, and decorated bowls used for serving food. Areas for grinding corn might be tucked into a corner. Alternatively, the roof of the living room or the plaza area in front of it could be used for such tasks. In the prehistoric pueblos it is not unusual to find entire rooms dedicated to grinding corn. These rooms usually contained several bins lined with sandstone slabs in which metates were placed for grinding.

Deeper in the household complex, either behind the living room or beneath it, are storage rooms where food and tools are kept until needed. Usually these rooms do not have fireplaces but might have shelves and bins. Some households have certain ritual responsibilities that include storing ritual artifacts (for example, clan **fetishes**) in these well-protected rooms.

The plazas have multiple uses, including ceremonial activities. Important **shrines** are found in certain plazas and, as mentioned above, kivas are also located in plazas. Religious groups or societies meet in kivas to conduct ceremonials, store some ceremonial objects, and prepare for the public dances and ceremonies held in the plazas. In addition to these kiva activities, the Hopi also weave cotton and wool in their kivas. Traditionally, weaving is done by the men. The blankets, dresses, kilts, sashes, string, and other pieces of cloth they weave are used in many ritual activities.

All the kivas in Hopi, Zuni, and the Homol'ovi ruins are rectangular. In the modern pueblo world rectangular kivas are found among Western Pueblo groups, while Eastern Pueblo peoples along the Rio Grande in New Mexico have circular kivas. This is an old architectural pattern, going back at least to the A.D. 1100s. Ruins in New Mexico and southern Colorado such as Chaco Canyon and Mesa Verde, have circular kivas, whereas ruins in the west like those at Homol'ovi and other sites along the Little Colorado River have rectangular kivas.

Modern Hopi kivas have roof entrances. Their occupants climb down into them using a ladder. The men sit on benches that line three sides of the structure while women sit on a larger bench (also called a platform) on the fourth side. These contemporary kivas may have a wood-burning stove for warmth, but in the past kivas had hearths and their roof entrances also served as smoke holes. To bring fresh air into the kiva and push the smoke out, older kivas had a ventilation tunnel on one side. To keep this fresh air from blowing on the hearth, a large stone or small wall called a deflector was placed between the opening of the ventilator and the hearth (see Figure 2). These features can all be seen in the reconstructed kiva at Homol'ovi II.

The Hopi trace family relationships through matrilineal clans, reckoning relationships through the mother's side of the family. All family groups belong to clans, which trace their origin to a common ancestor. In the contemporary United States, most people trace their family relations to both their mother's and father's relatives, and usually do not go beyond that in their classifications of kin. As a result they often inherit property from both sides. When they get married they desire to start a new home of their own and their in-laws on both side take turns visiting them there.

Among the Hopi, however, women own the homes and when they marry their husbands move in with them. Sometimes this means adding on another room or two in their suite of rooms in the pueblo. Personal property is inherited through the mother. Farming land, however, is not owned by a particular family of women but is instead communal property that is owned by the clans representing several related families. At harvest time, it was traditional for the clan members to work together on their lands to bring in everyone's crops.

Clans also own the knowledge, privilege, and artifacts used to conduct certain ceremonies. Clans usually have a ceremonial room used by clan elders to conduct ceremonies and store important ceremonial artifacts. Unlike kivas, these rooms are situated in the household suite of the clan's senior female. Single or multiple clans come together at scheduled times to plan and conduct ceremonies for the community. These forms of village and social organization were shaped over many centuries by an agricultural lifestyle focused around

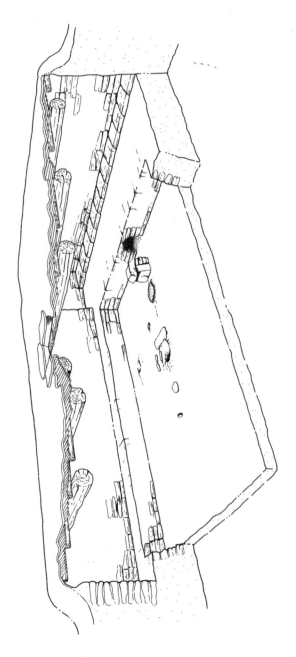

Figure 2. An Artist's Reconstruction of the Great Kiva at Homol'ovi II.

corn. Ritual and ceremonies are the fabric that holds these villages of desert farmers together.

THE HOPI KATSINA RELIGION AND THE HOMOL'OVI PUEBLOS

The modern katsina religion found in all Western Pueblo groups (Hopi, Zuni, Acoma, and Laguna) has its origins in the late decades of the 13th century among the populations who lived along the Little Colorado River.   The Homol'ovi ruins are especially interesting because they provide important clues to the early years of the katsina religion.

The Hopi believe that their ancestors as well as those of other nations entered into this world through an opening from the underworld near the Grand Canyon where the Little Colorado River meets the great Colorado River. Among the Hopi, when an individual dies, his or her spirit, or breath, travels to the underworld where it becomes a katsina.   Katsina spirits dwell part of the year in the home of the dead and part of the year among the pueblo peoples where they perform dances to bring rain. The katsinas return to the village in December and periodically participate in ceremonies and dances into July when they go back to the underworld through the San Francisco Peaks or the Grand Canyon.

When a Hopi man performs in a katsina ceremony he becomes one with the katsina spirit and can, if he dances hard and with a good heart, bring rain to the fields. While some katsinas come to the village to dance, others come in the form of clouds to provide the rain. Clouds form around the San Francisco Peaks, bringing moisture from these mountains to the mesas. As such, the San Francisco Peaks, like the Grand Canyon, have particular religious significance for the Hopi.

In addition to their rainmaking roles, katsinas also maintain order within the community by organizing labor parties to clean springs, disciplining unruly members of the community, and by leading war parties. When the U.S. cavalry attempted to make arrests in the Hopi village of Oraibi in the early 1900s, they were met by armed Hopi warriors and by Spider Grandmother and the Warrior Twins. During dances katsinas also redistribute food to reward and honor those living in the Hopi way as well as to supply food to those in need.

Because all members of the village have access to the katsina ritual, regardless of which clan they belong to, the ritual calendar unites all the people together. Pueblo religion is organized around a yearly series of public and secret ceremonies whose expressed goals are to keep agricultural fields fertile, bring rain when needed, and maintain social harmony in the village. Each clan plays a crucial role in this ceremonial calendar.

From an academic perspective this religious system would be classified as a form of ancestor worship. Deceased Hopi, rather than becoming dangerous ghosts, like the ancestors of the Navajo, or removing themselves to a distant world like the Christian Heaven, continue to be important members of the Hopi community, watching over their descendants and encouraging them to live proper lives. Katsinas have the power to reward those who live in harmony with their environment and to punish those who do not. This form of ancestor worship, focused on social harmony and rain making, was well suited to the social upheavals and environmental stresses of the late 13th century.

Beginning in the 13th century, pueblo peoples established large communities, in many cases creating villages that were larger than any that had previously existed. The common bond provided by the Katsina religion would have served to smooth social conflicts. By recruiting members from different clans to participate in religious ceremonies, the Hopi ensured that everyone had an important place in the ceremonies and in the village. Nonetheless, instances of violence at the site of Homol'ovi II suggest nonconformists or those who upset the balance of power in the village could be dealt with harshly. When drought or famine plagued a village creating social distress, such natural disasters might be blamed on someone with a bad heart. Responsibility for environmental problems might also fall on the ritual leaders who were primarily responsible for maintaining harmony between the community and the forces of nature.

The arrival and aggregation of immigrants in the Homol'ovi area, some from the east and south, others from the north, also corresponds with Hopi and other pueblo oral histories concerning the origins of the multi-clan villages. Modern Western Pueblo societies, such as the Hopi and Zuni, are composed of different clans who still trace their individual histories to many of the pueblos abandoned during the late 14th century. The Hopi oral histories speak of Homol'ovi and other pueblos inhabited before the villages occupied today were finally settled. One version of the occupations at Homol'ovi has been recorded as follows:[1]

> The Clans that went north from Palatkwapi stopped at one place and another...they went on until they came to the Little Colorado River near where the present town of Winslow stands. There they made a settlement that they called Homolovi, Small Mound, consisting of two villages, a larger one and a smaller one. The people of the Water and Sand clans occupied the smaller village. Sharing the larger village were Tobacco and Rabbit clans, and various others, including Eagle, Hawk, Turkey and Moon clans. After a time they were joined by the Badger Clan and a group that called itself the Reed Clan...then some other groups began to arrive from the direction of Myovi, the Rio Grande, in the east. Among them were the Fox Clan; certain people who as yet had no clan name but who would later become the Coyote Clan; and a branch of the Fire Clan. And, from time to time, still more groups drifted in from different directions. Thus Homolovi grew large and populous...
>
> One night in the northern sky there was a brilliant display of moving lights, and the clan leaders came together in the kiva to discuss the meaning of the event. They agreed that it was a signal for the people to go on with the migration that had stopped at Homolovi many years before. They announced to the people that they should prepare for a resumption of their journey...
>
> The largest part of the Water Clan and all other clans from Homolovi took the northern trail. They travelled across a barren land of sand, rocks, and buttes. They stopped and camped a while at a place known as Bird Spring. After that they continued travelling until they came to Little Ruin Mound, not far from where Walpi is today. They camped at that point and sent scouts out to see who might be living on the great mesa that was plainly visible.[Harold Courlander, *The Fourth World of the Hopis*, pp. 72-81]

---

[1]Presently, the Hopi Cultural Preservation Office recognizes the following clans lived at Homol'ovi: Water, Sun, Sun Forehead, Coyote, Tobacco, Rabbit, Sand, and Eagle.

From an archaeological perspective, a whole series of artifacts and activities are associated with the katsina religion, including dancers, plaza dance areas, food, and kivas where dancers prepare themselves and their tools for ceremonies. The katsina costumes are elaborate and composed of a number of objects, including various bird feathers, turtle shells, cotton kilts and sashes, bracelets, and fox pelts. There are many different katsinas with distinctive costumes and each requires a number of other artifacts to be complete. The cluster of artifacts that create the katsina religion in contemporary pueblos is quite distinctive and easily recognized. Finding archaeological evidence of these artifacts, however, is difficult. Many are perishable and would not survive long in archaeological deposits. Some are also used for decades or longer and are passed down from generation to generation. Only rarely would they be found in archaeological deposits. Finally, artifacts that are especially sacred are not simply thrown out in everyday trash dumps, but may instead be hidden when disposed of and, therefore, are not likely to be found by archaeologists.

As a result archaeologists have traced the katsina religion through its imagery on rock art, pottery, and murals painted on kiva walls. These katsina images occur in villages, like Homol'ovi I and II, that have large dance plazas and rectangular kivas. The earliest evidence of this religion suggests it began in the upper Little Colorado area and moved down river to Homol'ovi when these peoples founded the pueblos of Homol'ovi I, Homol'ovi III, Chevelon, and Cottonwood. It then spread up to the Hopi Mesas and returned as a more formalized institution in the 1330s with the founding of Homol'ovi II.

THE HOMOL'OVI PUEBLOS

As noted, there are seven pueblos in the Homol'ovi area. Four of the pueblos were numbered by Jesse Walter Fewkes of the Smithsonian Institution when he visited the area in 1896, and are emphasized here because of recent excavations in these particular pueblos. Two are on the west side of the river, Homol'ovi III and IV; two are on the east side, Homol'ovi I and II.

In the late 1200s, peoples abandoned the Four Corners region of the U.S. Southwest (the common borders of Arizona, Utah, New Mexico, and Colorado) and migrated to new areas, creating new and larger pueblos. About A.D. 1260 water tables began to drop and this was compounded between A.D. 1275 and 1299, when much of the Southwest experienced 25 years of reduced rainfall. Although rain fell each year, it was not consistent and undoubtedly created a time of hardship throughout the ancient pueblo world. Falling water tables and a reduction in the overall amount of rain not only led to crop failures but also would have thinned the ground cover. This could have initiated a cycle of erosion that would have further degraded the fertility of the land.

Even with all these environmental problems, areas like the Mesa Verde region could still have supported smaller groups of farmers. Such a change in the scale of communities, however, would have dramatically altered the social organization of these groups. How one organizes religious festivals, harvests, planting, marriages, or trade, is quite different in a hamlet of 12 to 15 people compared to a village of 100 people. Therefore, as people began to leave the Four Corners region, the reduction in the number of people living in a village would itself have motivated others to leave with them.

In such times of change and environmental stress, new religious institutions often develop in small-scale farming communities, and such was the case among the people living along the Little Colorado River and the Hopi Mesas. Evidence of religious elaboration includes polychrome (multi-colored) pottery decorated with parrots and masked figures, as well as large villages organized around plazas rather than great kivas. In addition to katsina iconography on rock art and kiva murals, other artifacts related to ceremonies such as piki stones (a stone griddle used to cook a thin corn-based bread called *piki*), and shoe pots (specialized cooking pots shaped like a shoe) have also been found in these villages.

The use of cotton in modern Hopi katsina religion for sashes, kilts, burial shrouds, and wedding blankets is well documented. The prominent depiction of cotton textiles in 15th century murals in kivas at Hopi villages suggests they were significant at an early point in the rise of this religion. Controlling the production of cotton would have served the ritual needs of the Homol'ovi peoples and given them an economic opportunity to exchange raw cotton or textiles to other pueblo communities involved in similar ritual activities. Excavations at the Homol'ovi sites have revealed abundant evidence of cotton being grown in the area during the 13th and 14th centuries.

It seems that the broad floodplain in the Homol'ovi area was a particularly attractive location for cotton farming. Cotton requires more water than corn and is less resistant to cold temperatures. As such, the Homol'ovi area would have been an ideal spot for those wishing to expand the production of cotton for trade and ritual reasons.

Homol'ovi IV

Homol'ovi IV was partially excavated by the Homol'ovi Research Program in the summer of 1989. It was founded by immigrants from the Hopi Mesas and was occupied between A.D. 1260 and 1280. Its approximately 150 small, masonry rooms (2m by 3m; 7ft by 10ft) were built in a step-wise fashion down the south and east sides of a small butte (see Figures 3 and 4). At the base of this butte was an open activity space containing prepared earthen surfaces. A small underground room was found in this area that may have been a corn grinding room. Several habitation rooms were uncovered on the hillside and at the base of the southwest side of the butte was a small masonry kiva.

The pueblo grew gradually, with new rooms added as needed. As the pueblo expanded so did its trade with peoples to the south. They imported sea shells, red argillite (used to make beads, pendants and miniature bowls), and finished tools of obsidian. These farmers probably traded their cotton in return. There is no evidence of the katsina religion's involvement in this initial cotton trade or the organization of this pueblo.

The architecture and ceramics found at Homol'ovi IV suggest that these people originated in the Hopi Mesas. There is even a

Figure 3. Excavations at Homol'ovi IV, 1989. (Photo courtesy of Homol'ovi Research Program, Arizona State Museum)

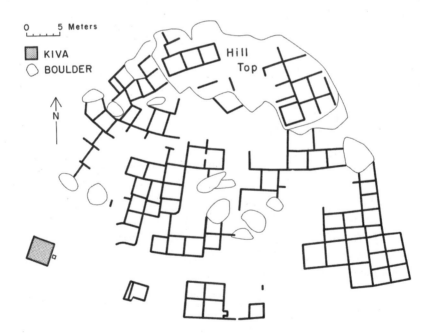

Figure 4. A Map of the Rooms at Homol'ovi IV.

pueblo two miles south of the Hopi villages on Second Mesa, called "The Little Giants Chair" (*Hoyapi* in Hopi) that is virtually identical to Homol'ovi IV. It, too, was occupied in the late 1200s and built in a step-wise fashion down a small butte.

Homol'ovi IV was occupied for about 20 years and appears to have been abandoned when people from the southeast moved into the area, establishing the Homol'ovi I, Homol'ovi III, Chevelon, Cottonwood Creek, and Jackrabbit pueblos. These pueblos continued the production of cotton, but on a larger scale, and probably incorporated this important economic activity into the developing katsina religion.

Homol'ovi III

About a half mile south of Homol'ovi IV, the pueblo of Homol'ovi III was constructed about A.D. 1280 in the middle of the floodplain. This was a smaller pueblo of 50 rooms, including large habitation rooms (2.5m by 4m; 8ft by 13ft), three rectangular kivas (one partially masonry, two earthen) and a masonry great kiva (8m wide; 26ft). Like Homol'ovi IV, this site also had an open space in front of the room block but did not have a formal plaza area (Figure 5). The ceramics are mostly orange wares often painted with two colors, black and white, and occasionally decorated with parrot images. Two imported Mexican macaws (parrots) were also found buried in a room occupied near the end of the site's use, sometime after A.D. 1350.

In contrast to Homol'ovi IV, the habitation rooms at Homol'ovi III were large and composed of both masonry and puddled adobe. The rectangular great kiva is also another striking difference. This type of kiva was common among pueblo people farther upstream to the southeast. It indicates, along with the distinctive ceramics and adobe architecture, that these people had immigrated to the area, traveling 50 to 100 miles (80 to 160 km) from the upper Little Colorado River, probably from the Silver Creek area which today lies between Show Low and Snowflake. Whereas Homol'ovi IV was occupied and then permanently abandoned, Homol'ovi III was abandoned due to increased flooding between A. D. 1300 and 1330, but was reused

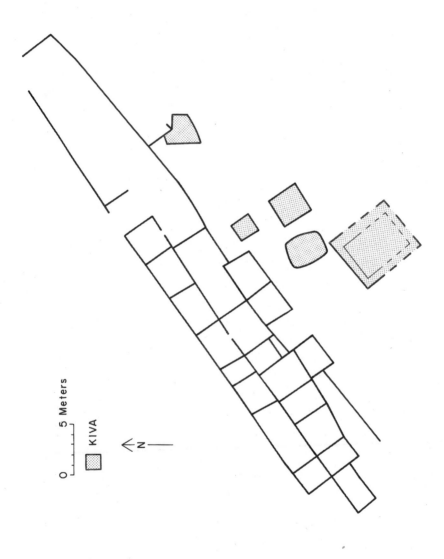

Figure 5. A Map of the Rooms at Homol'ovi III.

seasonally after the A.D. 1330s, presumably by the inhabitants of Homol'ovi I or II. The reoccupants burned the roofs of the earlier kivas, perhaps to purify the village before using it.

The floodplain locations of Homol'ovi III and IV, especially Homol'ovi III, indicate that the Little Colorado River was in a period of downcutting and lower stream flows during the late 1200s. This was a period of drought throughout the Colorado Plateau and the river would have been much more predictable and less likely to flood the broad plain during this time. As such it would have provided a safe area of farmland for cotton as well as corn, beans, and squash. After 1300, when the drought ended, and stream flows increased, the floodplain appears to have been more frequently inundated, making habitation there difficult, if not impossible. Flood-deposited silts have been found in the great kiva and several other rooms at Homol'ovi III, suggesting that flooding was the cause of its abandonment.

Homol'ovi I

At the same time that Homol'ovi III was founded, the larger pueblo of Homol'ovi I was constructed on a small rise on the east side of the river, just north of Sunset Crossing. Excavation of this pueblo began in 1994 and will continue for years to come. It was occupied between A.D. 1280 and 1380 and has over 700 rooms (Figure 6). Initially constructed on a slight hill, Homol'ovi I after 100 years of occupation had grown into a prominent mound visible for some distance. As rooms were abandoned and filled in with trash, new structures were built over them, creating a deeply stratified site.

One large kiva, several rooms, a plaza, and exterior spaces have been tested. This pueblo has large habitation rooms like those found at Homol'ovi III, but they are arranged around several plaza spaces-- at least three small plazas, 2 to 3 rooms wide (8 to 10 m; 30 ft) and a large square plaza, 10 to 11 rooms wide (30 m; 100 ft). Excavations at the site have revealed a variety of architectural forms and materials. Three kinds of adobe walls have been found, including rammed earth, post-reinforced, and mold-made adobe bricks.

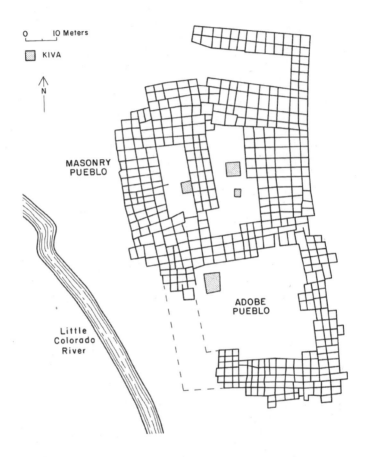

Figure 6. A Map of the Homol'ovi I Pueblo.

Masonry walls were also present. Although there were many masonry walls, very few wall stones can be seen today on the surface of the ruin. Mormon settlers building the nearby settlements of Sunset and Brigham City removed many of the stones for use in constructing their forts in the 1870s.

The types of pottery found in the uppermost **strata** at the site are dramatically different from those found in earlier deposits. Orange-colored pottery, produced locally, and red-colored and white-colored pottery, imported from the Silver Creek area, occur in the lower strata but are almost totally replaced by yellow pottery in the upper layers. The yellow pottery was traded down from villages in the Hopi Mesas.

Homol'ovi II

The site of Homol'ovi II was partly excavated in 1984 and between 1991 and 1995. It has three large rectangular plazas; the eastern one is open on the south side. This site was occupied between A.D. 1330 and 1400. In addition to about 1200 rooms, there are approximately 40 kivas constructed in its three plazas; the largest kiva is located in the central plaza (see Figures 7 and 8). This kiva, along with several storage and habitation rooms, has been reconstructed and can be seen from the sidewalk that guides visitors through the ruin. Almost all of the decorated pottery found at Homol'ovi II is Hopi yellow ware. Pottery specialists at the Smithsonian Institution, in Washington D.C., have analyzed the formal properties of the clay in several of these pots and have determined they are identical to the clays surrounding the large historic Hopi village of Awatovi, 60 miles to the north. Other artifacts and architecture at this site also tie its inhabitants closely to the Hopi that once lived at Awatovi (this village was abandoned in A.D. 1700), and other villages on the Hopi Mesas.

There are two painted kivas at Homol'ovi II linked to the religious symbols of the katsina religion. One has a mural of the San Francisco Peaks painted across its western wall. The other depicts two dancers wearing cotton kilts; these dancers may represent katsinas. Most of the shrines, rock art panels with katsinas, and check dam features found during the Homol'ovi Survey occur within a mile of this pueblo. With the founding of Homol'ovi II, the other pueblos appear to have reoriented their trade networks toward the Hopi Mesas. The distinctive Hopi yellow ware pottery (Figure 9) replaces most of the earlier red and orange ceramics. This pottery continues to feature the bird designs found on the earlier ceramics and incorporates stunning katsina faces that link it symbolically to the katsina religion (Figure 10). Presumably all the Homol'ovi pueblos were trading their cotton to the Hopi Mesas in exchange for yellow pottery.

It appears that people on the Hopi Mesas and the upper Little Colorado River both wanted to colonize and develop the floodplain of the Homol'ovi area in order to grow cotton. In all the large

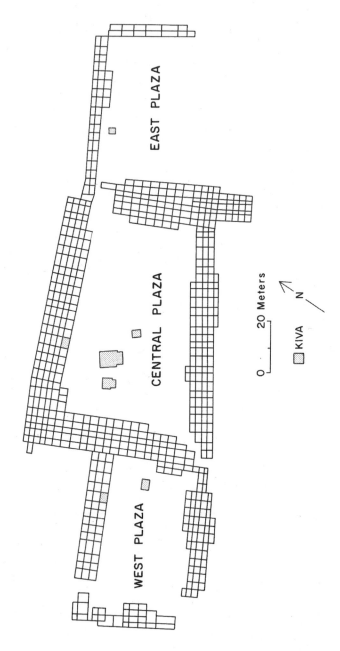

Figure 7. A Map of the Homol'ovi II Pueblo.

Figure 8. An aerial view of Homol'ovi II (photo by Terrence Moore).

Figure 9. Jeddito Yellow Ware Ceramic Vessels.

Figure 10. Jeddito Yellow Ware Bowl from Homol'ovi II With a Depiction of a Katsina.

Figure 11. Petroglyphs (rock art) near Homol'ovi II. (Photo by Sally Cole)

Homol'ovi villages, the **flotation** samples have contained high frequencies of cotton seeds.

The Hopi, as represented by Homol'ovi IV, were first to the area, but may have departed when a larger number of immigrants moved in from the southeast. The Hopi returned in large numbers later with the founding of Homol'ovi II and seem to have successfully re-established Hopi dominance in the area. This pueblo, unlike the earlier Homol'ovi IV colony, appears to have a strong katsina presence, including formal plazas, murals, ritualized kiva abandonments, katsina rock art, and shrines.

At the site of Homol'ovi II the ceremonial deposits are quite distinctive and suggest that the katsina religion was rather formal at this site. In addition to the painted kiva murals of dancers and the sacred San Francisco Peaks, every ceremonial structure excavated to date was ritually abandoned through burial or burning. It is clear that the distinctive ritualized construction and uses of these buildings was continued through their abandonment. Unlike the abandonment of other rooms, the filling and burning of these kivas resembles burial rituals that are usually reserved for people. Whole pots were sometimes intentionally buried in the kivas when they were abandoned. Several of the burned kivas also contained burned cotton textiles sacrificed when the kivas were intentionally destroyed. In at least two kivas there is also evidence of violence, perhaps related to internal conflicts in the village.

A major source of conflict within the pueblo cultures of the U.S. Southwest is the belief in witches, who are seen as threats to the harmony and physical health of the community. Witchcraft is not unique to pueblo societies, however; it is seen in many cultures around the world. In the 17th century, witchcraft was an important element in the history of Salem, Massachusetts. Pueblo peoples are always on the lookout for such evil people. Today, witches are ostracized by the community, but in the recent past they were sometimes killed. The killing of a witch would not have been an unusual function of a developing religion, especially in a village the size of Homol'ovi II. In pueblo villages today, ritual leaders are often given the responsibility of judging and punishing witches.

All of these pueblos were abandoned by A.D. 1400. Stream flow information suggests one of the worst episodes of flooding in the northern Southwest occurred in the 1380s, followed by a devastating decade-long drought. Such flooding and drought, in conjunction with more than a hundred years of farming in the area, may have simply made the area no longer capable of supporting large villages. The Hopi legends describe the Homol'ovi peoples and others coming to the mesas after a great flood caused by a giant water serpent at the legendary site of *Palatkwapi*. The late 14th century flooding at sites like the Homol'ovis may relate to this history of the clan migrations to the Hopi Mesas.

RECENT HISTORY OF WINSLOW AND THE SURROUNDING AREA

Between 1876 and 1880 a series of Mormon colonies were established along the Little Colorado River and Silver Creek drainages. In 1876 the settlements of Obed, Sunset, Brigham City, and St. Joseph were founded, followed in the next year by Woodruff, Snowflake, Taylor, and Show Low. In 1879 St. Johns, Springerville, Eagar, and Alpine completed this period of Mormon colonization (see Figure 12).

Both Brigham City and Sunset were located on the floodplain of the Little Colorado River, approximately a mile north of where Interstate 40 crosses the river. Brigham City had a medieval appearance, constructed as a rectangular fort. Although in hindsight it is clear that danger from local Native Americans was minimal, the first settlers feared that they might be attacked. Brigham City's stone walls were eight feet high and on its northeast and southwest corners were bastions that provided lookouts and the ability to fire down on invaders approaching the walls. It contained a school, gristmill, tannery, pottery firing kiln, and a blacksmith shop. Some excavations have been conducted at Brigham City by the Arizona State Museum and local volunteers. The settlement at Sunset (see Figure 13), located on the floodplain, was washed away by the river many years ago. The Sunset cemetery, however, still stands on a sandy terrace

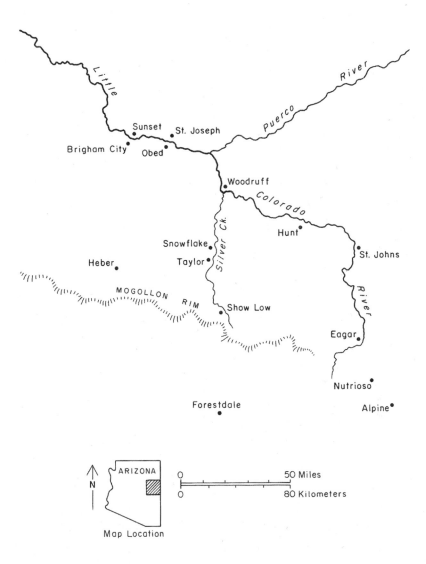

Figure 12. Mormon Communities of the Late 1800s in Northeastern Arizona.

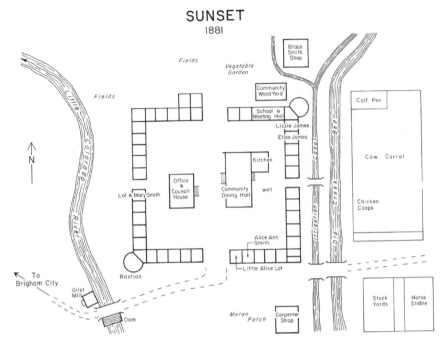

Figure 13. The Mormon Fort of Sunset, ca. 1881.

overlooking the Little Colorado River, and can be visited on a trail from the Homolovi Ruins State Park Visitor Center. The Mormon settlers dammed the river and attempted to irrigate the large floodplain, but each year the river flooded badly, destroying their crops, dams, and irrigation canals. These settlements were abandoned by the early 1880s.

The history of Winslow itself and that of Northern Arizona is intertwined with the rise of the Atchison, Topeka and Santa Fe Railroad. Historians generally agree that Winslow was named after General F. Winslow, President of the St. Louis and San Francisco Railroad. This company also owned half of the Atlantic and Pacific Railroad, which founded the town of Winslow in 1881.

When the A.T. & S. F. began in 1863 it was given ten years to reach the Colorado state line from Kansas. Few had faith in its prospects; a lot of money had to be raised and tracks had to be laid. Completion of the railroad took almost exactly ten years, but the tracks reached Colorado and the railroad received its charter for more land. Continuing to expand, the rails moved westward with the goal of completing a transcontinental route across the middle of the country. The Southern Pacific, already in California with its own transcontinental route in the south, initially frustrated the Santa Fe line. Nonetheless, the Santa Fe followed the 35th parallel across New Mexico and Arizona and acquired its own rails in California. This transcontinental route passed through Winslow.

When the Winslow terminal was founded just south of Sunset Crossing, F. G. Demerest opened the first hotel, a tent, adjacent to the new terminal. Like earlier pueblo immigrants, these pioneers took advantage of the good water and the Sunset crossing to establish an important trading node on the railroad that connected Winslow with points east and west. In January the following year, a Post Office was opened with U. L. Taylor as postmaster. At this time Winslow was the end of the line for the railroad. The canyon lands west of Winslow were particularly tough to cross. El Diablo Canyon, 26 miles west of Winslow, was perhaps the foremost obstacle the railroad engineers faced. The bridge constructed there took six months to complete; it stood 222 ft high and 560 ft long (see Figure 14).

By 1893, the Santa Fe rail network was the largest in the world; it stretched from Chicago to the Gulf of Mexico and across the west to San Francisco and San Diego. Winslow thrived along with the Santa Fe. Cattle and agricultural produce were shipped on the trains to markets in the east. The luxuries and entertainments of the modern world also came to Winslow.

A new train depot was constructed in 1897, including upgraded facilities for luxury dining in one of the many Harvey house restaurants that distinguished this rail system. In the late 1890s, F. T. Aspinwall was clamoring for the electrification of Winslow, and so in 1898 Winslow's Electric Light and Ice Manufacturing Company filed articles of incorporation. Accompanying the new depot and electrification of Winslow was the construction of Winslow's opera house, which was begun in 1897 and completed in 1899. Its first

Figure 14. Railroad Bridge over El Diablo Canyon. (Photo courtesy of the Navajo County Historical Society, Old Trails Museum, Winslow)

production was *The Banker's Daughter*. The Baseball Association constructed a field and officially opened it with a game on July 4th, 1900. In that same year, the first black boxing champion, Jack Johnson, held a prize fight at the Navajo Hotel in downtown Winslow.

As Winslow moved into the 20th century, it was a culturally diverse community composed of Anglos, Native Americans, African, Hispanic, and Chinese Americans. Attracted initially as laborers for the railroad, the Chinese, known as "celestials," opened laundries, restaurants, and other service industries. Other minority populations found employment opportunities in this boom town. A community of African Americans came from Louisiana to work in a Winslow saw mill. Although quite civilized by the second decade of the 20th century, Winslow still had the flavor of a wild west town with 14 brothels and 7 saloons with casino gambling. The community was divided along ethnic lines that were seldom crossed socially. The Hispanic community, for example, lived south of the railroad tracks, had its own community meeting hall, and generally did not attend performances at the Opera House.

Willa Cather, the novelist, had a brother living in Winslow as a railroad worker. She lived with him for a time getting to know the town and surrounding sights. Literary scholars have argued that several of the characters and places described in her novels, *The Song of the Lark* and *The Professor's House,* were drawn from her adventures in Winslow during the teens.

As with so much of the history of Winslow and Northern Arizona, the railroad provided a model of social relations among the peoples living in Western America. Fred Harvey, an immigrant Englishman, had the sole concession for the restaurants and hotels throughout the Santa Fe rail system. He established a high standard for these establishments, making his hotels and eateries the envy of travelers and merchants the world over. In the 1890s he replaced all his restaurant's male waiters with "Harvey Girls" (Figure 15). These were unmarried, white women who signed contracts of 6 to 12 months to provide a civilizing atmosphere in the Harvey houses. They had black-and-white uniforms, and lived in dormitories adjacent to the rail

Figure 15. Harvey Girls at the First Harvey House in Winslow. (Photo courtesy of the Navajo County Historical Society, Old Trails Museum, Winslow)

depots. They had to remain unmarried while working for Harvey, but many of these women, at the ends of their contracts, married local ranchers or railroaders and settled down in towns like Winslow. One such Harvey Girl, Cecil Creswell, became a colorful local character and has been profiled in *Arizona Highways* magazine (October, 1995).

In 1920, Lorenzo Hubbell, Jr. , son of the famous Ganado Trader, Lorenzo Hubbell, bought a trading post in Winslow from the Robinson family (Figure 16). This post, like others along the railroad, sold Native American handicrafts, tools, and other supplies. This particular store also served the young entrepreneur as a warehouse for his growing business in the region. To move heavy objects from the basement to its loading docks, the first Kimball Brothers elevator west of the Mississippi was installed in this building. Although no longer a trading post, the building still stands today on Second Street. From 1985 to 1991, it served as the field laboratory of the Homol'ovi Project as well as a temporary headquarters for the Homolovi Ruins State Park.

Throughout the 1920s, trade in Native American arts and crafts became a significant side business of the Harvey company and was expanded to include tourist excursions, or "detours," led by another group of Harvey women. These were college-educated white women, who were given crash courses in Southwestern geology, archaeology, and history to equip them as attractive and well informed "detour" hostesses. To complete their image, these hostesses were dressed in wool skirts and velvet Navajo-style blouses (Figure 17). From Winslow, tourists could travel to the Hopi Mesas, Meteor Crater, and the Petrified Forest. To accompany its expanding tourist interests in northern Arizona and New Mexico, the Harvey Company built a series of luxury hotels from Santa Fe to the Grand Canyon. The last and quite spectacular of these was the La Posada Hotel in Winslow, completed in 1930 (Figure 18). This hotel cost over $1 million and was designed by Mary Colter, who designed several of the Grand Canyon's hotels and lodges. She also designed a set of fine china for use in the Harvey houses modeled after the beautiful black-and-white designs of prehistoric Mimbres pottery found in southwestern New Mexico. Today these pieces are treasured collectibles. The La Posada was operated until 1957, when it was sold to the railroad. The

building is currently being acquired by investors for the city of Winslow who want to restore it to its former Harvey House glory.

Although the Great Depression of the 1930s cut into Winslow's hopes for tourism, other forces also undermined the railroad's control of the tourist industry. The 1930s witnessed the growth of commercial air travel in the United states. Charles Lindbergh, already carrying mail across this region of the country, was given the job of surveying the western United States for new transcontinental flying routes. Because he was a frequent visitor to Winslow and a national celebrity, a wing in the La Posada Hotel was set aside and named for him. In those days, flights stopped more often, and he established Winslow as layover for service and refueling. No less a personage than Pope Pius XII, when still a Cardinal, stopped in Winslow in 1936 while en route to San Francisco.

During the Second World War, hundreds of thousands of soldiers, and others on war business, filled the rail depots of the Santa Fe. The elegant dining halls served by Harvey girl waitresses became quickly antiquated. Huge numbers of people had to be fed, quickly and cheaply. The luxurious Harvey standards and racially segregated practices could not be upheld as the needs of the war effort brought minorities into military and civilian jobs. Finally, after the war, car travel along U.S. Route 66 took most of the passenger traffic away from the railroad. As a consequence, the tourist industry, once centered on the railroad, shifted in the postwar years to Route 66 and other roadways.

In 1978, the two lane Route 66 was replaced by the larger Interstate 40. This highway skirted the downtowns that Route 66 had passed through and, as a result, many hotels, restaurants, gift shops, and other businesses suffered. Nonetheless, new stores and restaurants have sprung up around the new highway and the opportunities for tourism have never been better. Winslow is still centrally located for visiting the Hopi Mesas, the Petrified Forest, Meteor Crater, and, of course, the ongoing explorations at the Homolovi Ruins State Park.

Figure 18. La Posada, Winslow, designed by Mary Colter and completed in 1930.
(Photo by Richard W. Lord)

STUDYING THE PAST

Archaeologists are often asked how they recreate history from what amounts to old trash (such as broken pots, fallen buildings, and food waste). The remainder of this booklet provides a brief introduction to the ways archaeologists working in the Homolovi Ruins State Park retrieve and organize information from archaeological **sites**.

The term *archaeology* is derived from Latin and means the study of the ancient world. Although often confused with paleontologists who study ancient fossil life (including dinosaurs, giant ferns, and extinct sea creatures), archaeologists are social scientists interested in the human past. Unlike other social scientists such as economists, sociologists, or historians, archaeologists depend on the study of **artifacts** to reconstruct human history. We all live in a world defined by objects--houses, cars, hammers, food, clothes, furniture, fuel, bibles, santos, and so on. Almost anything people do in some way involves artifacts. Archaeologists, therefore, reconstruct the past by understanding in detail how artifacts were used in human behaviors. Computers, calculators, and electronic artifacts dramatically shape the way we work, educate and entertain ourselves today. In the same way, water jars, corn grinding stones, and cotton looms were important in the daily lives of the prehistoric people who lived in the Homol'ovi area.

As a result, every artifact holds many clues for archaeological investigation. This book, for example, holds much more information than simply the text you are reading. It is an artifact that contains many traces of our contemporary society. The paper from which it is made comes from trees cut down and processed by people in the Northwest United States. It was written in Tucson using a computer manufactured in Japan. It was printed and bound by other people working in Tucson.   These events date its manufacture, and its published copyright provides the date of its earliest use as a book in American society.

Archaeologists track artifacts across geographic regions. The distribution of this book will depend upon you. Will you take it to Flagstaff, Alabama, or maybe Germany? How far you take it and what season you are traveling could tell an archaeologist something about your behaviors. Eventually, you may give this book to a library or sell it to a secondhand bookstore; perhaps you will pass it along to your children with your other books. Understanding these behaviors would help an archaeologist reconstruct your age, wealth, and perhaps occupation as well as understand the use of this Park as an education and research center.

Ultimately at the end of this sequence of events this book will end up in the archaeological record at a specific point in time at some specific place. If it survives the acids, rodents, worms, and fungi of that lonely spot it may someday reenter the stream of human activities. If we are lucky, perhaps it will be found by a future archaeologist, providing that archaeologist with a glimpse into our lives and knowledge in the late 20th century.

To reach you, this book has already passed through many peoples' lives. From this point forward it will pass through yours and perhaps many more. In each of these moments in its life-history as an artifact, this book participates in a behavior that captures a small part of our society. These events leave traces on the book and direct it toward another set of human hands.

Wood ➜ Printed Book ➜ Your Book ➜ Inherited Book ➜ Discarded ➜
Archaeological Specimen A.D. 2525

Figure 19. This Book's Possible Life-history

Objects like the Egyptian pyramids or even the glamorous hotels of Las Vegas may reveal more spectacular traces of human behavior than others, but all artifacts, from paper clips to the space shuttle, provide archaeologists with clues for reconstructing how people made a living, what they ate, where they traveled, what they enjoyed and what they found sacred. Archaeologists study the past by learning how ancient peoples made, used, and discarded artifacts.

Archaeologists excavating in the Homolovi Ruins State Park travel into the past by reconstructing these uses of artifacts. At Homol'ovi, archaeologists are particularly interested in understanding why ancient Pueblo peoples migrated to this area and built, lived in, modified, and abandoned several large pueblos between A.D. 1260 and 1400. As a result, they have studied the natural resources available in this area and how the Homol'ovi people used them to create many distinctive artifact life-histories (for items such as architecture, food, cotton, corn grinding and cooking stones, and pottery), including those involving ritual, particularly the katsina religion.

HOW TRACES OF BEHAVIOR ARE MEASURED FROM ARTIFACTS

Archaeologists employ four general types of measurements for studying artifacts (Figure 20). Any object or group of objects can be counted (frequency measures). Their locations in a site can be recorded (spatial measures), as can their associations with other artifacts (relational measures) in those places. Finally, their many physical characteristics can be observed (formal measures). In their analyses archaeologists combine these various measures to infer the past activities involving an artifact or group of artifacts .

For example, volcanic glass (known as obsidian), like old-fashioned soda bottles, fractures into razor-sharp pieces that make excellent knives, scraping tools, and arrow points. Its sharpness and ability to break in controllable ways are measurable formal properties. Created by volcanic eruptions, obsidian only occurs in specific places on the landscape (a spatial measure) like the lava flows around the mountains near Flagstaff, 60 miles west of Homol'ovi.   Not surprisingly, obsidian artifacts occur in lower frequencies in the Homol'ovi sites than in sites closer to Flagstaff. Within a large pueblo like Homol'ovi II, wornout obsidian tools occur in trash deposits where they are associated with other wornout artifacts (relational measure). In contrast, whole obsidian artifacts, such as arrowpoints, may be found in association with ritually abandoned pots in ceremonial rooms, like kivas (another relational measure).

Whole artifacts (formal property) are fun to find but a broken artifact (formal property) can be an equally important clue for

Figure 20. Homol'ovi Artifacts (clockwise from the top): large, corrugated cooking/storage pot; grinding tools, mano (top) and metate (bottom); decorated serving vessels, two bowls and a ladle; stone tools, four arrowpoints and one knife or spear point; shell bead necklace; miniature decorated jar; stone mortar for grinding foodstuffs or pigments. (Photo by Richard W. Lord)

understanding past activities.   For example, ceramic bowls are sometimes broken (formal property) after a feast and placed together (relational property) in special ceremonial trash piles (spatial property).   If one were not aware of these possibilities, a pile of broken bowls might appear to be a disappointing heap rather than the traces of an important sacred event.

THE ARTIFACT LIFE-HISTORY APPROACH

Some archaeologists employ life-history studies, pioneered by researchers at the University of Arizona, to organize measurements of artifacts into exciting bits of information about the people who used them. The life-history approach is a favorite of Homol'ovi archaeologists because it allows them to compare known artifact life histories in contemporary pueblo cultures like the Hopi to life histories of artifacts from the ancestral Homol'ovi pueblos. Every artifact has a life that begins when its raw materials are gathered together (materials such as obsidian, clay, sand, and wood) and that continues through other stages such as manufacture, use, reuse, and recycling into other artifacts.

Eventually, all artifacts, wind up in an archaeological deposit where they endure the weather, burrowing animals, and other processes that may move them from where they were originally laid down. These processes also cause artifacts to decay, changing their formal properties. For example, a wooden artifact, like a digging stick, may turn pink if attacked by a fungus, or simply decay into a dark stain in the dirt. In the Homol'ovi ruins, small mice, packrats, and other rodents often dig into the soft trash deposits and move artifacts up and down, mixing earlier and later deposits. Looters, not concerned by the destruction they are causing, also mix deposits, but on a much larger scale.

Raw Material ➜ Manufacture ➜ Use ➜ Reuse ➜ Recycling ➜ Disposal ➜
Natural Processes ➜ Found in Excavation

Figure 21. Generalized Life-history for Artifacts

Although archaeologists find artifacts at the end of their life histories they usually want to know about earlier stages. Each of these earlier segments was a moment when someone used the artifact. To make connections between the end of an artifact's history and earlier segments, archaeologists study artifact life-histories in the present as well as in historical cases. From these known histories they can determine which formal, frequency, relational, and spatial measures will best link the end of an artifact's life history to the earlier behaviors of interest.

For example, the oral traditions and historic records of Hopi people making, using, and disposing of clay cooking pots provide archaeologists with clues concerning how to interpret the whole and broken cooking pots they find in the Homol'ovi ruins. Because cooking pots are used over an open flame for long periods, these activities leave dramatic traces in the formal properties of these objects. These pots usually have jar rather than bowl shapes because this allows them to more effectively hold heated liquids. They are not usually painted because their outsides become sooted and food residues coat their insides. They are often thicker than decorated serving bowls in order to retain sufficient strength in the face of repeated heating and cooling.

Eventually, however, heating and cooling take their toll, and the pots break or crack. At this point they might be mended, but it is more likely that the pots would be thrown away with other household trash such as animal bones and wornout stone tools. Alternatively, their life-histories might continue through a series of new activities. For example, on the Hopi Mesas, observers in the 1800s noted that many cooking pots, lacking their bottoms, were used as chimney tops on the roofs of pueblo rooms (Figure 22). From this point forward, the lives of these pots would parallel those of the rooms to which they were attached. If the room and the pueblo were abandoned, the pot would probably remain in place until the roofing wood rotted and the structure collapsed. At that time the bottomless pot would probably break into more pieces and wind up in the fill of the room mixed in with the roofing beams, grasses, and mud.

Figure 22. Last House on Walpi. (Note use of ceramic vessel as part of chimney. Photo courtesy of Arizona State Museum, University of Arizona. Negative #33742 by Forman Hanna, ca. 1920-30)

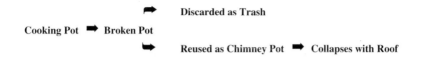

Figure 23. Alternative Cooking Pot Life-histories

Archaeologists can also read historical descriptions about how Hopis use grinding stones. These stone tools are used to grind corn, process pigment, shape wooden artifacts, and manufacture other stone tools. Ground stone artifacts are manufactured of different types of stone collected from various sources, such as the sandstone outcrops that occur in the Homol'ovi area. Some of these tools spent their entire life-histories in the village, but a smaller number were taken to agricultural fields, rock art sites and other places where they were used.

Ground stone artifacts, because they are difficult to carry, seldom left the village. Metates, a large and heavy corn grinding stone, would have been a relatively stationary artifact. If metates were taken out of the village they were usually left at an activity area ready to be used when needed.

When metates wear out, which can take decades, they are often reused as pueblo wall stones or broken up to construct slab lined hearths. As a result, archaeologists find them in collapsed walls, burned in fire pits, or in trash mixed with the ash of a cleaned-out hearth rather than in the places where they were used to grind corn. Nonetheless, the surfaces of corn grinding stones have been ground smooth and can be used to identify earlier milling activities.

Because oral traditions and historical descriptions of people making, using, and disposing of artifacts are almost never complete, archaeologists themselves also go out among living peoples to study artifacts and record their life histories. This kind of research is known as *ethnoarchaeology*. Some ethnoarchaeologists from the University of Arizona, for example, study the Kalinga peoples of the Philippines because these people still make and use pottery in everyday activities like prehistoric pueblo societies. The long term goal of the Kalinga

Project is to apply what is learned about these life-history events to pots recovered from archaeological sites like the Homol'ovi ruins.

Experimental archaeology is another strategy archaeologists can exploit for understanding artifact life histories. Through experiments they can explore why specific artifacts are used in specific ways and how these activities alter the formal properties of the artifacts. Archaeologists interested in grinding stones can fashion metates using different types of stone and then measure how these experimental tools perform in different tasks. Experiments have shown, for example, that grinding stones made of basalt are effective for reducing dried corn kernels to small granules, but finer-grained sandstones are better for making a corn meal flour.

Experimenters can also measure the different patterns of wear that different tasks leave on the same materials. For example, through experiments, archaeologists have demonstrated that a hand-held mano of fine-grained sandstone could be effectively used to dehair hides, break up dried meat, or shape wooden objects. By grinding these different substances on manos, made from identical Moenkopi sandstone materials, archaeologists have identified microscopic differences in the wear patterns these tasks leave behind on the artifact.

ARCHAEOLOGICAL SURVEY

When archaeologists want to investigate a previously unstudied area they have three primary questions: Where are the artifacts? How did they get there? and When did they get there? Answers to these basic questions allow archaeologists to choose, depending on the goals of their research, which sites to dig and which to leave alone. Knowing what archaeological information is out on the landscape is also important when dams, highways, power lines or other potentially destructive construction projects may be proposed in an area. Often these projects can be adjusted to avoid damaging or destroying archaeological sites. If not, archaeologists can at least excavate the sites before they are destroyed, preserving the valuable information they contain.

Often farmers, ranchers, and other local people can point archaeologists to concentrations of artifacts. To get more complete information, however, archaeologists usually employ a systematic search called a **survey**. Archaeologists employ various techniques when surveying areas like the Homolovi Ruins State Park. Some have conducted "windshield" surveys, driving along dirt roads looking for human-made mounds and architecture, while others have sought more detail from the back of a horse. Some have even flown slowly over the landscape in helicopters, spotting sites from the air.

Walking over the landscape, although time consuming, is the most thorough technique. The walking survey of the Homolovi Ruins State Park and surrounding areas, for example, took 5 summers to complete. Survey crews examined approximately 33 sq. miles (85 sq. km). Walking in groups of 4 to 6 persons spaced between 15 m and 25 m apart, 100 percent of the Park was examined, and everything from isolated artifacts to entire pueblo villages was recorded and mapped.

The Homol'ovi Survey was designed to provide a more complete picture of the environment and culture history of the Park. The surveyors' study of the environment and geology of the area enriched our knowledge of the prehistoric peoples' sources of fuel, construction materials, fertile soils, and the naturally occurring animal and plant life. The sites they found represent the remains of more than three thousand years of human activities. They identified several earlier sites where people had constructed small pit house hamlets and pueblos. These **habitation** sites, however, were far less common than sites representing other activities such as farming, the making of rock art, and the gathering of resources. In total, over 500 locations of artifacts outside of habitation sites were found by the Homol'ovi Project surveyors.

Some of these non-habitation sites occurred at places on the landscape where resources could be gathered. Flaked stone artifact scatters were found on the terraces where cobbles would have been picked up and tested for making cutting and scraping tools. There were also sites among the Moenkopi and Shinarump sandstone outcrops where stone suitable for use in pueblo walls and as ground stone tools was quarried.

Other sites found during the survey provide indirect evidence of activities such as farming. Contemporary Hopi people often farm in the sand dunes that surround their mesas. These sandy areas often lie over hard-packed clays that water has difficulty penetrating. Rainwater percolates several feet into the sand and gets trapped above the clay; the covering sands keep it from evaporating. As a result, these dry-looking sand dunes can actually provide a moist soil for crops, like Hopi corn, that have long root systems. Hopi and other southwestern tribes also farmed in the sandy deltas of small arroyos, where summer rains running in the arroyo could be diverted into and away from fields as needed.

In the sand dunes of the Park there are scatters of ground stone, ceramics, stone alignments, hearths, and small temporary shelters representing temporary agricultural field camps sometimes called *field houses*. A typical field house site might contain a small structure, a hearth, and a scatter of surface debris--perhaps generated during a temporary visit. The ceramics in these sites represent water and storage jars that might have been used in corn and cotton fields to water the plants and collect their produce. Discarded stone hoes are also found in higher frequencies in these field camps.

Figure 24. Artifacts Interpreted as Hoes from the Homol'ovi Area. These typically occur in areas assumed to be used for farming. (Photo by Helga Teiwes, Arizona State Museum).

In fact, the large broad valley on the east side of the river separating the large pueblos of Homol'ovi I and Homol'ovi II was named Hoe Valley in recognition of the high concentration of these types of artifacts that occur there. The sand dunes in this valley had more hoes and temporary structures than any other of the Park's side valleys

The Homol'ovi area is also rich in rock art (Figure 11). The more than 500 rock art panels scattered throughout the Park and adjacent areas visually document 3000 years of Homol'ovi history. On the exposed Moenkopi and Shinarump sandstone cliffs and buttes near the site of Homol'ovi II, there are areas with **petroglyphs** depicting masked figures, animals, plants, spirals, and other abstract images. The making and use of rock art are often associated with ritual activities in modern pueblos. Contemporary Hopi carve masked figures to represent katsina spirits and often symbolize clan names by drawing the animals and plants corresponding to their names, such as the lizard clan or the bear clan. Other carved images are pecked to bring fertility to young women.

RECOVERY TECHNIQUES

To begin reconstructing the past, archaeologists must keep track of the contexts where they recover artifacts. These contexts contain all the spatial, frequency, relational, and formal traces they will need to reconstruct earlier stages in an artifact's life history.

Because the place an artifact is found represents the last activity it participated in, archaeologists record these spaces in as much detail as possible. In the movies archaeological tools often include whips, guns, and binoculars. In reality archaeologists depend upon trowels, cameras, pencils, carpenter rules, recording forms, and computers.

Typically, archaeologists spend 10 months analyzing and writing for every 2 months of excavation. The information they use during those long months includes forms, maps, and photographs compiled in the field. Archaeologists have forms on which they record measurements of the length, width, and depth of the deposits yielding artifacts.   On these forms they also describe the type of dirt (sand, clay, silt) and other distinctive qualities of the deposits, such as color, abundance of artifacts, traces of burning, and rodent disturbance. *Features*, like stone walls, hearths, earthen floors, and pits that cannot be removed from the dirt without destroying them, are mapped and photographed.

These forms and maps preserve information about archaeological deposits which can now be dramatically displayed with the graphics programs of today's powerful personal computers. Archaeological excavation destroys deposits, and so the context of an artifact can only be recorded once. Maps, therefore, must be accurate and as detailed as possible to preserve information for future generations.

To document the contexts of artifacts successfully, archaeologists must know how they entered the archaeological record. Such discard events create a layer or deposit of artifacts--called a *stratum* (the plural of stratum is "strata"). The study of strata, called *stratigraphy*, is a critical part of understanding how artifacts got to their present locations in the ground.

By mapping layers of artifacts in three dimensions (Figure 25) and keeping the artifacts within these layers separate, archaeologists can gauge how different activities led artifacts to different strata in a site. Sometimes these differences are simply the result of time. Layers of artifacts that are deposited upon other layers are usually more recent in time than the layers they cap. This is called the *Law of Superposition*. In a trash dump, a basket of charcoal and ash may be emptied on the pile one week, creating a layer, and a few days later an identical basketful may create a similar layer over it. The life-histories of the artifacts in these two layers may be nearly identical except for the fact that the layers occurred at slightly different times.

In addition to the Law of Superposition, archaeologists have other techniques for measuring the passage of time. Dating ruins by the age of the trees used in their construction was pioneered in the U.S. Southwest. **Dendrochronology**, or "tree-ring dating," relies on a known pattern of tree-ring widths to determine when a tree was cut down and used in the past. Archaeologists can also measure the decay of radioactive carbon atoms in once-living materials (such as wood,

Figure 25. Mapping a Wall at Homol'ovi II. (Photo courtesy of Homol'ovi Research Program, Arizona State Museum)

cotton fabric, and bone) and then determine how long ago they died. This technique is termed **radiocarbon dating**.

At Homol'ovi we have very few tree-ring dates because cottonwood trees, the most predominant roofing wood used in the Homol'ovi pueblos and pit houses, cannot be used for tree-ring dating. We use radiocarbon dates, but the margin of error for this kind of dating is generally too great for the precision needed for dating the occupations in the Homol'ovi pueblos. The most precise technique is termed *ceramic cross-dating*. Many of the ceramic artifacts found in the Homol'ovis have been dated elsewhere, where they occur in association with tree-ring dates, and we can use these dates to build a relatively detailed chronology for the Homol'ovi ruins.

Archaeologists' reconstructions of the past can be confused or limited if the original strata are destroyed or mixed by vandals. At Homol'ovi II, for example, looters have excavated large holes in the ruin, knocking down walls, removing objects, redepositing other artifacts, and generally scrambling the patterns that were present before their vandalism. Even if they returned all the artifacts to Park archaeologists, much information would still be lost forever. Archaeology is not simply about finding artifacts; the *context* of an object is the critical issue. Looted artifacts are accompanied by no forms, maps, or photographs. Regardless of how pretty the objects may be, they cannot take one into the past in the way a well excavated, thoroughly recorded assemblage of artifacts can.

Anyone who has participated in an excavation quickly realizes that there are many ways to record layers of artifacts. In the early years of this century, many archaeologists simply shoveled through them and gathered what they saw by hand. In this fashion they were able to excavate hundreds of pueblo rooms in a field season. With more precise research questions and a deeper appreciation of the information contained in artifacts and their contexts, modern archaeologists now use more detailed techniques for recognizing and studying archaeological deposits. To meet these challenges they now pass the dirt of strata through screens (see Figure 26). One-quarter inch mesh is a common size, but deposits of small beads and chips of stone can require smaller mesh sizes.

Figure 26. Excavations at Homol'ovi III with staff and Earthwatch volunteers. Note the many activities: troweling, mapping, and screening. (Photo courtesy of Homol'ovi Research Program, Arizona State Museum)

For example, a kiva at Homol'ovi II had a particularly rich series of strata containing hundreds of shell beads *(Nassarius moestus)* that would have slipped through a 1/4-inch screen.   To ensure that these artifacts were not missed, an 1/8-inch screen was employed.   Shell beads are extremely rare at this site, and so it was critical to use recovery tools that would not miss them. When these shell artifacts were counted in the laboratory, it turned out that they came from a necklace composed of at least 223 beads traded up from the Gulf of California.

Screen size alone cannot ensure the successful recovery of artifacts. If the screen mesh is too small, it cannot efficiently separate the dirt from very small artifacts. As a result, other techniques, such as flotation, pollen, and microartifact sampling, have been developed to recover small objects. **Flotation** is an especially useful technique for retrieving plant remains like cotton seeds, charcoal bits or corn kernels that might occur in a prehistoric hearth.

Plant pollen preserves well in many archaeological contexts and provides clues about the quantities and types of plants people used in the past. Pollen samples are taken from contexts in which plants may have been in use, including floors of rooms, storage bins, niches, and hearths. Microartifact samples are also taken from similar contexts and examined under a microscope in search of objects such as chipped stone, ceramics, or animal bone that are less than 2mm in length. Because pollen and microartifacts are so small, it is conceivable that they may have escaped the cleaning up that accompanies most activities. Thus, they would occur in strata such as outdoor surfaces, room floors, and storage bins.

CONCLUSION

As you now know, the work of archaeology can be slow and it is far from glamorous. Although we dream of time machines, archaeology is our only true window on the remote past. Everyday, looters and vandals destroy that past before we ever get a chance to know it.   Your enthusiasm and interest will help us protect what is left of that precious heritage so that it can be preserved for future generations.

Perhaps you can imagine the fields of cotton and corn in late fall, just before the villagers came to take in the harvest. In the plazas of the large villages, you might envision the kivas where the cotton was woven and dance preparations were carried out.

The Homol'ovi area has been a cultural crossroads for thousands of years. Your visit here has contributed to that stream of human history. We hope you will return in the future to see what exciting artifacts and history Park investigations have unearthed. If you do return, expect to see more than simply rocks and dirt, for the remains of pueblo and pit house villages and the environment that these ancient people exploited so effectively will also be accessible.

SUGGESTED READING

Adams, E. Charles
1991 *The Origin and Development of the Pueblo Katsina Cult.* University of Arizona Press, Tucson.

Adams, E. Charles, editor
1995 *River of Change: Prehistory of the Middle Little Colorado River Valley.* Arizona State Museum Archaeological Series No. 185.

Adams, E. Charles, and Kelley A. Hays
1991 *Homol'ovi II: Archaeology of an Ancestral Hopi Village, Arizona.* Anthropological Papers No. 55. University of Arizona Press, Tucson.

Carlson, Vada and J. Rodriguez
1981 *A Town Is Born.* V. Carlson and J. Rodriguez, Winslow, Arizona.

Cole, Sally J.
1992 *Katsina Iconography in Homol'ovi Rock Art, Central Little Colorado River Valley, Arizona.* Arizona Archaeologist No. 25. Arizona Archaeological Society, Phoenix.

Courlander, Harold
1971 *The Fourth World of the Hopis.* Crown Publishers, New York.

Ferg, Alan
1992 Brigham City Fort - 1991 Excavations. *The Society for Historical Archaeology Newsletter* 25(3):33.

Poling-Kempes, L.
1989 *The Harvey Girls.* Paragon House, New York.

Reid, J. Jefferson and David E. Doyel
1986 *Emil W. Haury's Prehistory of the American Southwest.* University of Arizona Press, Tucson.

GLOSSARY

Artifact: Any object that has been used or altered by human activity; including tools, architecture, or the landscape.

Dendrochronology: The study of how the growth patterns of trees, "tree-rings," correlate with time. Roofing beams are most commonly dated by this method (see Reid and Doyel book in the Readings).

Fetish: An object such as a concretion, figurine, or statue believed to possess supernatural power.

Flotation: A technique for recovering small seeds, other plant parts, bones, and artifacts. The soil from a feature, such as a firepit, is poured into fine-mesh screens in a large container of water. Materials that have been burned will float and can be skimmed off; other materials are recovered from the fine screens.

Habitation site: A place where people live and do domestic activities on a regular basis, including eating and sleeping. Habitation sites can be contrasted with places where people hunt game, farm, gather raw materials, or prepare ritual objects.

Hopi: (pronounced *Ho' pee*) A pueblo tribe numbering about 12,000 living primarily on a reservation in northeastern Arizona, 60 mi north of Winslow. Their ancestors lived at Homol'ovi and in other parts of the Colorado Plateaus. The Hopi language is a member of the Uto-Aztecan linguistic family.

Katsina: (pronounced *kat see' na*, also spelled **Kachina**, pronounced *ka chee' na*) An ancestral spiritual being that brings rain and social harmony to pueblo villages. There are many different katsinas in the pantheon of the Hopi and other pueblo tribes.

Kiva: (*kee' va*) In Hopi, this terms means "underground room." Archaeologists almost always use the term *kiva* to describe underground ceremonial rooms in prehistoric pueblo sites.

Mano and metate: Tools used together to grind food, minerals, and other materials. The mano is held in the hand (*mano* is Spanish for hand) and rubbed against the metate which remains stationary.

Petroglyph: An image pecked into a rock. **Pictographs** are painted onto the rock. Both are commonly referred to as "rock art."

Pit house: A house or dwelling that is partially excavated into the ground. Often these appear as large pits filled with organic matter and other trash when archaeologists find them, hence the term *pit house*.

Plaza: A communal space bounded by buildings in a village or town. Both ceremonial (katsina dancing) and economic (trading, corn grinding) activities take place in plaza areas.

Pueblo: (*pwe' blow*) A series of masonry buildings with many rooms and often with multiple stories that form a village or town. Pueblos resemble contemporary American apartment buildings.

Radiocarbon dating: A dating method based on the known rate of decay of the radioactive form of carbon (carbon-14) to determine the age of organic materials such as plant parts, hair, and bone.

Shrine: A feature or construction in a ceremonial place or building that serves as a contact point with the sacred. Shrines are often used to make offerings and prayers and to give thanks.

Site: A cluster of artifacts or features on the landscape resulting from human activities.

Strata: (plural of *stratum*) A stratum is a discrete layer of artifacts and dirt deposited in a site.

Survey: The locating and recording of archaeological sites, usually by systematically walking back and forth over the landscape. Surveys are often conducted as the first step in research when investigating previously unstudied regions.